THE LIZARD CATCHERS

Peter Thabit Jones

THE LIZARD
CATCHERS

Art by Nick Holly

Cross-Cultural Communications
Merrick, New York
2006

Acknowledgment is due, with thanks, to the editors and publishers of the magazines and newspapers, anthologies and Teachers' Resources, and others listed on pages 61-62.

Cloth Edition/ISBN 0-89304-864-X
Paper Edition/ISBN 0-89304-865-8

Editor-Publisher: **Stanley H. Barkan**

Cross-Cultural Communications
239 Wynsum Avenue, Merrick, NY 11566-4725/USA
Tel: (516) 868-5635 / Fax: (516) 379-1901
E-mail: cccpoetry@aol.com
www.cross-culturalcommunications.com

Welsh Poets #1

First Edition

Designed by Tchouki

Printed in Bulgaria by **ANGO BOY**

in memory of
my grandfather and grandmother
and for
Vince and Annie Clemente
and Stanley H. Barkan

CONTENTS

CAJO'S FARM

The sawmill cut into the day,
Its work a grinding wooden noise;
Logs screamed into halves,
Into log families.

Old Cajo and his sons let us hang around,
The labouring sounds pig-squealing into our heads.
We bagged the chopped stick like giant chips,
We swept the floor's mess of yellow snow.

The machine's teeth were like a shark's;
A disc's serrated threat, a metal grin.
Biting into the bark, it spat pine dust.

We loaded the lorry
And took to the estates, the lonely homes;

The Cajo sons safe inside the cab,
While we sat on a mountain
Of blocks and bags:
Moving above the speeding cars.

THE LIZARD CATCHERS
(for Molly)

Tattooed on the rocks in the midday sun,
They were hieroglyphs we understood.

Behind the boy-tall grass, we slyly sat
As patient as pyramid statue-cats.

The moments burned; the flying rooks were vultures;
The sky was blue, some brittle clouds in heaven.

Like 'palm crocodiles', like playtime dinosaurs,
They basked in a freedom known aeons ago.

As dry as Lazarus just from the tomb,
Legged snakes, rest lodged in them as sweet as dust.

As still as lizards photographed, like taut thoughts,
The smoke of autumn's drug dreamed through their world.

One by one, we hurried to seize our catch;
The lizards darted, swimming through the grass,

Discarding their tails tugged off by clumsy grasps.
Then we claimed the rocks and blessed them with our laughs.

THE BOY AND THE LION'S HEAD

(In Swansea, South Wales, on Kilvey Hill,
near a place called Crymlyn Woods,
there is a rock shaped like a lion.
It is known locally as the Lion's Head.)

One Sunday, I crossed Kilvey Hill
And saw a strange, thin man sat still,
By the rock shaped like a lion,
Above Tir John Power Station:
As private as a Nazi camp.
His rough clothes labelled him a tramp.
He beckoned me to join him there,
But I was frozen like a hare.
"Come touch the Lion's Head," he said,
"Shout 'Great white eye you're red and dead',
And the stunned sun shall loudly fall
Down on the town's brown streets that sprawl,
By the sea." His voice frightened me.
It unlocked fear like a key.
His grin was like a killer's knife;
He stood up—would he take my life?
I hurried through the gasping grass;
My groin felt stabs of pain like glass.
The sun bled; I almost stumbled:
Behind me, the stranger mumbled.
"Come touch the Lion's Head," he said,
"Shout 'Great white eye you're red and dead'."
I ran above the quarries that fell
Sharply like a falling boy's yell.
I stepped down the sloping heather:
Port Tennant crept through mad weather!
I passed a ditch—a witch's bed—
Go touch the Lion's Head, it said.
The trees spat birds, stone horses ran,
As I fled from that dreadful man.

Over the wall, into our back,
I hammered our door. Crack. Crack. Crack.
"The sun is falling, Mam," I said.
"Okay, son, but we must be fed."
I told my dad the tragic news.
"Go away! I'm fixing this fuse."
I stared coldly at our fire:
The glaring coals shouted, "Liar!"
I went and stretched out on my bed,
Touched an imagined Lion's Head,
The magic words I softly said
And closed my eyes from falling red.

WELLER

We were waiting behind an upturned car—
Tyreless, windowless and freckled with rust—
On a rough track across the rubbish tip
At the back of Tir John's red-bricked stacks pointing up
Like something out of Lowry's drab past.
Only us and a bloke—stick-poking for rare
Finds in smouldering rubbish—were around.
Weller was staring down the barrel of his gun;
I was holding a tobacco tin
Of lead slugs in the cold palm of my right hand.
We were waiting for starlings, scribbling on
The blue surface of the sky, to fly down then
Strut on the track; and for hair-raising rats
To slink up the bank sliding down to the bog—
With its black, smelly water and sharp reeds
Huddling like millions of sky-stabbing swords.
We heard a distant bang like a clapped, ballooned bag;
We looked towards Morris Farm—rabbits
Popped-up like fairground targets on his plagued hill.
"That's a winner," Weller whispered, grinning.
We had wasted half of the promising day,
Rummaging in rubbish gone cold. I found a small,
Scorched tea-pot and threw it down moaning:
"I've steeped it too long!" Then Weller gave out a cry—
He had found a half-burnt men's magazine.
We sat on a tea-chest, curious as cats;
We made out assorted breasts, legs and hairs
And one full-length Negress stretched out on white furs.
We then shot at bottles and filled tins with dots;
We shot at gulls high as the mad sun.

Bored with waiting behind the old car,
I nudged Weller. Frowning, he said, "Look, there's a crow."
He lifted the gun—his cheek kissed its smooth wood—
He closed one eye and pulled the trigger;
The crow fell from the fence. I ran and I saw
The black belly boasting a jewel of blood.

THE BOY

The boy, when ill, would listen to
The whispers in the parlour room;
He'd hear his grandma's distant words:
The window showed November greys.

He'd colour books with heavy hand;
He'd hear the cars park in the street,
The tied-up dog's cold, winter growl.
He'd draw, like invalids, the trees.

The day contained him in his world,
Above the place where language lived
Like fish that bubbled out round sounds.
He'd lie like someone kissed by death.

Beneath the blankets, in his bed
(The smell of art, the waxy sticks;
The morning's drug that was ill-health),
His head was warm with harem thoughts.

He'd think of breasts and hair and thighs,
Remember those unloved, untouched,
Until he rose like Lazarus
And walked into the breathless sea.

The colours grew, the old voice flew
Towards the hill, the trees stripped bare;
The tall girls howled like forest wolves
And stars stuck in the frosted air.

MY GRANDFATHER'S RAZOR
(in memory of my grandfather)

I used his razor once;
Aged fifteen, face fluff-haired,
I locked the bathroom door.
I soaped my tanned boy's face
And held the loaded tool.
I recalled how he shaved,
Pillow-propped up in bed:
The bed in the parlour.
His sunk shoulders towelled,
His brush tickled the soap,
Until his Auschwitz face
Had a beard of snow;
I held the square mirror.
The razor ploughed and rasped,
His hand trembling slightly;
And he always shaved twice.
Sometimes, he nicked his neck,
Wrinkled as a turkey's,
And I watched his blood come.
It always made him smile;
And cigarette paper
Blotted dry the blemish.
The ritual over
He swilled clean his smooth face:
Hair, like iron filings,
Tide-marking the white bowl.
That first night, when I shaved,
Afraid of the new blade,
I removed *more* than hair:
As downy as a girl's.
For I knew, as I worked,
My hand trembling slightly,
I was shaving away

The softness of boyhood;
I would leave the bathroom
Feeling more like a man.
And my reflection smiled
When the blade caught my skin:
For from my snow beard
I watched adult blood come.

BURNING WASTE
(for Gareth and Katharine)

The bonfire flares,
Shredding the black night.
The wooden bones crack.
Smoke, salt-white, departs,
Thinning, vanishing
On its self-made tracks.

The wax faces of children
Are buttered with firelight.

GARDEN OF IVY
(for Hilary)

Ivy has taken over our lives:
A new house and an overworld of green;
Clinging—like thick, grubby, bark-skinned cobwebs—
To old pipes, walls, and the 'rag-and-bone shop'
Of someone else's dead life. It seems sly;
Entangling itself throughout the rotten,
Wooden skeleton of a large glasshouse;
It covers an old mangle heavily—
Like a bamboo-woven mat. The dead, brown
Tentacles are brittle as baby bones:
They biscuit-snap. Above, white flowers snow
And a dirty shower of big, green moths.
The limbs of disorder? Or nature
Left to ooze its joy? It grasps the high walls
Like provocative art: a seaman's rope
Snaking on the dry surface of cement.
It has branches as thick as a man's wrist;
I hack, with an axe, into this jungle
Of garden shame; I saw its brown tendrils,
Revealing a gaping, tattered whiteness.
I am its sweating slave; its dust peppers
My salted face. My slicing and tugging
Release the ruined, rusty riches;
Captured under its green revolution.
But someone else must have loved it; needed
This waterless aquarium of weeds.
And I think of lonely Edward Thomas,
Liking tall nettles but disliking man.
It hangs, unruly, above my smallness:
Like frayed, green curtains and arthritic sticks.
The rough invasion is now retreating.
Now the garden is free of oppression
(Though I feel no pride in my ruthlessness);
Just a bunch of green moths clutch a bald wall.
Stretching up, I pick off the bold parasites;
For they say it comes back with a vengeance.

19

GOWER DELIVERY

For the last hot hour or more,
I have been carrying boxes
To the top step, the ninth step,
Of the front door of this exclusive,
Seaside, mock Miami Beach hotel.
Once again, up into the rancid
Back of my van; checking cold boxes
Of scampi, cod, mixed vegetables,
Plaice, hake, French fries and slabs of meat,
Against the journey-crumpled,
Delivery-note. The frozen foods
Thawing in the furnace of the van.
Once more, I struggle back up the
Crunching, gravel path. A woman
Guest, as desirable as an iced lager,
Smiles from a high, sun-demanding balcony.
Two bold children, their ice-cream cones dripping
In the mischievous heat, hurry
Down the quaking path to the crowded
Beach: the dead sky shrouds sea and sand.
Back to my sea-blue van—with the painted,
Smiling fish and short-haired, apple-cheeked
Butchers on its doors. The sun has gone mad!
I guzzle the last sour drops
Of lukewarm Coca-Cola in my can,
Wipe my wet brow in my shirt-sleeves
And stoop down to re-tie a limp shoelace.
Glancing up at the balcony,
I find my golden Eve has gone.
Then the front door opens and she comes out,
Her tanned body testing her bikini's strength.
Smiling, she moves to the car park
And gets into a dark red sportscar.
I return to the burning hotel,
For a man's unruly signature.

MODRIS

Modris sits on the warm doorstep,
Wearing a pullover knitted
By his blind sister.
He grins at fresh girls clip-clopping
In high, platform shoes
Down the sun-blurred street;
Tut-tuts at the old Indian
Doctor's sons playing
Football against a garage door;
Accepts homemade cake
From the young wife across the road;
Gives children hot mints;
Asks me about Keats.
Goes in about ten in the night.

I live three houses away.
Midnight, I can hear him coughing.

VOLUNTEER WORK: SPECIAL NEEDS

Plants seem to share a language that is green;
On rows of wooden tables, they are displayed
In their silent conversation, in their prayer.
I stare at the dense wealth of garden growth,
The velvet wax health of the gorgeous leaves.
The roomy glasshouse breathes in heated air.

Four students, each one deaf, re-pot small plants
And fill big pots with black earth from a trough.
They pat the baby leaves into the soil,
With a tender pride that's really not for boys.
They shoulder bloated bags to make more space;
They box the dirty rags, stake dripping fronds.

A helper brings in a girl, limp in wheel-chair;
The tightened face laughs, as the deaf boys greet her.
One shows the careful work, the pot-trapped plant.
In damaged speech, she screeches for a chance.
They hold the plastic trough up to her hands
Bent, like broken shovels, on hopeless wrists.

She scoops the soft dark soil, the humble goodness;
It falls on pathetic legs, her stiffened slacks.
She persists and is noisy at some success;
We lift her up to see the mess of crumbs.
She signs to me that she *has* potted seeds;
She holds the plant and thumbs the perfect leaves.

HARRY PUSHED HER

Harry pushed her;
He pushed her around;
Before school, after school;
On weekends.
He pushed his sister;
He had no friends.
He pushed her: school holidays
And Christmas time.
The children always
Sang their made-up rhyme:
'Harry push her, push her now!
Harry push the crazy cow!'
Harry pushed her without strain:
Through snow, sunshine, wind and rain.
She smiled strangely
And never said a word.
He pushed for years—
It was so absurd.
Harry was twelve;
His sister twenty-three.
Harry never had a childhood like me.
Harry pushed her without a care;
He pushed his sister in her wheelchair.

LUNCH IN A CITY PUB
(for Vincent and Caroline)

They come and go, the people I don't know.
They purchase their drinks and sink into chairs;
Some read creased papers: "Suns," "Mails" and "Mirrors."
I listen to soft conversations grow
And watch how carefully the barman pours
A bottled beer. Does my staring show?

Sleet blisters the window. A young girl laughs
At a friend's fetish for raisins and nuts;
They tease each other like a pair of cats:
It hurts my eyes to see how much she loves
His pose. She stands and goes to the toilets.
I give my attention to other lives.

What thrives in city pubs is loneliness,
Concealed inside the odd person sat still,
Whose despair is as real as the smell
Of others in the room; whose chilled Guinness
Helps to forget the loud-voiced threat of all
Those crowded in a smoky happiness.

One enters and one leaves: blind to my stares.
Who bears pressing success? Who lost good bets?
Exciting and dull, people come and go;
Their lives, to me, as blank as fields of snow.

HOME

I never won your games of Cat-and-Mouse,
The arsenal of your words, so hot and cold.
Dying in your bed, you would snipe at me.
A target for your mind: a cadet to scold.

And yet there was joy in your trench-dark eyes,
As the hostilities stopped across our Somme,
And your stories gripped like a borrowed book
When you laughed like a lad on the road to home.

THE PROTEST

Because of the creaking of floorboards
I have sneaked down into the kitchen

Because of the mugs of cold coffee
I have pushed open the parlour door

Because of the stillness of the furniture
I have wandered out into the night

Because of the garage door open
I have run breathlessly down the drive

Because of a silent, empty street
I have drifted into a police station

To report my parents missing.

PSALM FOR THE TWENTIETH CENTURY
(for Lani, Colum and Anna)

Blessed are the hills that the acid rain kills.

Blessed are the trees dying of disease.

Blessed is the flower sucked of its power.

Blessed is the grass destroyed by the gas.

Blessed is the soil that we stupidly spoil.

Blessed are the clouds, the chemical shrouds.

Blessed are the rivers now they are sewers.

Blessed is the sand like mess in my hand.

Blessed is the sea that is oiled and filthy.

Blessed is the sky where the sick winds fly.

Blessed are the hens in their holocaust dens.

Blessed is the grain grown only for gain.

Blessed is the fruit that we daily pollute.

Blessed is the meat that we cannot eat.

Blessed is the bird that is no longer heard.

Blessed is the seal that the knives unpeel.

Blessed is the air that our lungs cannot bear.

Blessed is the town that we bulldoze down.

Blessed is the child that the city drives wild.

Blessed is the man and his 'live-for-now' plan.

Blessed is the Earth as we plunder its worth.

BUNKER FROG

A mildewed king in my bunker of wood!
Lifting up two palettes (my makeshift lids),
I'm startled by this repugnant squatter:
Frozen ugly on my neatly-stacked pile.
How did this alien get inside here?

What should I do? And why don't I like it?
Probably my schoolboy's cold-skinned fear
Of a moist street on a dark evening
With its pavement stones that turned suddenly
And horribly into vile, hopping frogs.

In those callow days, one bonfire night,
One boy trapped a frog in a biscuit tin
And filled it with sizzling, blue-tongued bangers.
Amongst the explosion of mad laughter,
He placed on the lid: petrified stranger.

I was too afraid (unlike the others)
To look into the grinning boy's Auschwitz;
To see the mess of childhood cruelty:
The pulp of spawned blood, the mustard vomit.
I tried to pretend we did not do it.

"Let's go and find more frogs!" somebody cried
To the small conspiracy of bullies.
Why didn't we leave the creature alone?
Let nature's oddity go its own way?
My mind broods on that mob entertainment.

What should I do? I don't want to kill it.
I just want to move this unwelcome guest,
As repulsive as fresh, dog excrement;
This squashed-looking, slimy thing that is green:
Chameleon trying to hide its gold.

It has such batrachian dignity.
Its bulging old-world eyes sulk over thoughts
Of wetter places beyond the bunker.
Its lemon throat pulses with yellow life:
As constant as a heart; its one movement.

Unlike Lawrence did with his famous snake,
I take a stick and attempt to launch it
Into a warm and shadowy corner;
This smug-headed ornament of dull brass
With verdigris. This princely visitor.

LAVACOURT, WINTER, 1881:
A PAINTING BY CLAUDE MONET

1.

Winter, for you, is blue;
And the cottages, too, are denim sky.

Why do you bring such cold to our eyes?
Why bring us the purest colour
That's morning-new?

Even snow
('The leprosy of nature'—
According to you),
Is a blemished flooring
Powdered with blue.

All is as stark as graveyard view;
The blue outside a shadow.

It's the ice in our lives, sharp and true;
The splinter of death that grey time knew.

2.

This is the other side of *A Field of Poppies;*
Your summer scene of tranquil France,
With its rash of redness daubing the grass
And your strolling family captured lovingly.
This is another season;
The broken mind's darkness,
The winter settling in the head,
The heart's bone of blue.
This is when Camille, your wife and model, was dead
And you were bankrupt
(Selling your paintings to pay your dues).

3.

They say you planted your easel
In the frozen river,
To achieve an effect such as this,
A canvas that chills where human grief grew.

Later, you talked of painting
That which is 'impossible to do';
You who loved colour,
'My day-long obsessions, joy and torment'.
And your lily ponds of Giverny come to mind;
Those floating flowers of clustered snow,
Those impressive blurs of crusty white,
In the mirroring calm water of your garden;
Those last paintings as cold as this hardened blue.

SNOW, GUITAR, LORCA

The fingers relieve the guitar of its sorrow;
Outside, the snow is slowly melting:
It's coldness has lingered in our hearts for too long.
A frozen song is slowly melting.

In the cellar's candled dark, you pour bottled wine;
Two girls hold hands but one is crying:
Have the crowd's ghosts of smoke flung grey salt in her eyes?
The guitar says the world is crying.

The man utters the sad words that shadow our dreams:
The laments of Lorca are living.
Outside, the town that was wintered is darkening;
Each face is strained with its own living.

The empty bottles of wine are guards of dark glass;
The bar is closed and people leaving;
The ashtrays display their grey gardens of nightmares;
The man with the guitar is leaving.

We say our goodnights on a street crusted with snow;
The world of white has started fading;
Our cold fingers relieve our hearts of their sorrow;
The red wine's warmth is slowly fading.

THE PRIEST-POET: R. S. THOMAS

Now I'm beginning to know
Your considered dark,
The contradictions in your work—
The wasted words you threw

At fools, who were always looking
For a mirror to reveal
Themselves; until they only revile
You for disliking, not for liking

The sweet birds, the peasanted hills,
The silences that your God left
In the mind's uneasy loft
That housed their heavens and their hells.

GARDEN OF REST, SAINT THOMAS CHURCH: SWANSEA
(for my grandmother)

It is the eighth day into May
And the cherry blossom flowers,
Holding up its pink fall of snow,
In front of the tall, church tower:
Boasting its clock—round, black and gold.

My grandmother dead a full year,
I pot some garden daffodils,
As my daughter toddles away
And demands me to 'Walk, Dad. Walk'.
She smiles with the freshness of Spring.

There is no elegy today,
No new grief on the playing wind.
Only my daughter nagging me:
'Walk, Dad. Lani walk. Walk, Dad. Walk'.
And this beautiful, pale-pink tree.

A shower of delicate thoughts
Frozen above me and my child;
An open umbrella of growth;
It hangs, pure, almost weeping.
The season's pink resurrection.

I crumple the newspaper sheet
And grasp my daughter's holding hand.
I watch as her small foot covers
A fallen flower on the path,
Crushing the soft, pale-pink petals.

WATCHING THE SEA: SWANSEA BAY
(in memory of my father)

When it comes to the sea, we never learn;
It can turn a ship over, crumble cliffs,
And scald a city with its cold, bitter blue.

The mariners of paid order, time splits
Our habits; it loosens the watching moon
And the hell of the sea smothers the air.

It is we who dwell on death, not the sea;
It has no thoughts, it has no gnawed memory,
Only the sulk of its hulking energy.

The fondling waves fool the eager bather,
The playboy's yacht, the fishing-boat and tanker:
The sea covers man's commerce and pleasure.

Becalmed, the sea wears the strangest wreckage:
Chapel roofs, school-gates, and gorgeous forests.
On its ancient bed, the drowned cultures rot.

We take to the stillness of the sea, filled
With our water-grabbing dreams and childhood's gulp
Of its salty liquid at some tourist bay.

If we dwell too deeply, the sea's horrors
Anchor down each fathomed thought heavily;
For there is nowhere for the sea to go

But over the waiting land, the planned dreams,
The great schemes of centuries and histories,
Drowning humankind in a second Flood.

THE COLD COLD CORNER

'Father, Father, I dread this air
Blown from the far side of despair,
The cold cold corner . . .'
—from "The Child Dying" by Edwin Muir,
Collected poems (Faber and Faber Ltd.)

(for Mathew)

1. Bereavement

Your head is full of trees
And the leaves have fallen.

Your eyes are full of lakes
And the water's frozen.

Your ears are full of birds
And the songs are stolen.

Your mouth is full of skies
And the clouds are ashen.

Your heart is full of fields
And the grass is barren.

Your soul is full of hills
And the paths are broken.

Your life is full of caves
And the dark is open.

2. February World

February world is a cold world;
February world is cold.
The wind comes across the field of graves
To winter body and face.

February world is a grey world;
February world is grey.
Like nightmares of snow, the sky shows clouds
That move in a heavy mood.

February world is a hard world;
February world is hard.
The grass is as coarse as leather shreds;
The cross stands in clinkered sod.

February world is a dulled world;
February world is dulled.
Leaves are flung to the wind like regrets;
Grief is a re-opened cut.

February world is a sad world;
February world is sad.
The dead child, the father who survives;
The flower pot clogged with ice.

February world is a dry world;
February world is dry.
The day is a funeral of thoughts;
The past is a frozen knot.

3. Mathew

On Sundays, we go to attend to his grave:
The large, paper cornet foaming with flowers;
And our eyes as dry as the surrounding stones.
His smile and small darkness are vinegar
Memories stinging the cut cord of our living love.
His white cross stabs the formal grass. His photos,
Wordless elegies, inhabit my wallet.

4. No Language

There is no language to say I miss you.
Yet sometimes in the working day
(When worries enter my being
More quickly than the appropriate words),
My body movements freeze
And my mind seizes the one thought,
And I stare like a man fooled by it all:
Like a fox crossing a long field,
Suddenly stopping dead
To stare back at the cornered past:
The ghost of a fox hanging in its head.

5. A Cross

I once made a cross for my dead son's grave.
I purchased two pieces of perfect wood;
Unskilled and unsure, I laboured slowly:
Marking, sawing and chiselling the joints.
I thought of other fathers shaping wood
Into well-made cots and nursery chairs:
The prepared gifts for their lives' new fullness.
I sharpened its longest length to a point.
My brown hands soon held the reason for Christ.
I painted it white and then let it dry;
With a small, fine brush and a pot of black,
I added his name, his age, R.I.P.,
And the September date of his young death.
I went up to his grave with fresh flowers
And I hammered the cross into wet ground.
It stood, declaring his eight months on Earth;
It stood, coldly stabbing the emptiness.

6. Remembrance

I bury you softly in thoughts like snow;
I wear my grief, my black flower of pain.
My thoughts are prayers that can never reach home;
I tend to your grave in the cold of cold rain.

A CLOCK TICKING AND AN OLD MAN

A clock ticking and an old man,
Who's slowly dying in bed;
A young boy sat by a fire,
The old man dead in his head.

A clock ticking towards darkness,
A window crying with rain;
A young boy warming his cold hands,
An old man shrouded in pain.

A clock ticking and a young boy
Undressing his thoughts of night;
The old man imagining death
Softened by feminine light.

A clock ticking and a fire
Burning to a grave of grey;
An old man in his dark chapel;
A young boy too cold to pray.

A clock ticking and an old man,
Who's slowly dying in bed;
Recalling the young boy's fire
That burnt, like truth, in his head.

A clock ticking and a young boy
Hearing, in darkness and rain,
The cry of the old man in him,
The truth of forthcoming pain.

THE GREEN BIRD
(for Vince and Annie Clemente)

You were born glowing
And when the green bird
Landed on you
It left all its songs.

But you preferred silence,
The raindrop of a thought
Shining on a leaf,
A shadow statued in prayer.

The crowds waited like a river,
The poetry of your soul
Would silver the desert,
The aeons of poverty.

You sent them a stone,
They built you a tomb.
You pointed to the moon,
They broke all their mirrors.

Words shone like stars in your mind;
They were not to be sung.
Silence surrounded you
Like the perfume of flowers.

You breathed in the universe,
As you shed each moment
As stiff as a snake
That's mesmerised by light.

On the edge of morning,
They found you perfected.
You'd made it to god.
They cut down a tree.

You died in the darkness
But glowing inside:
The bright songs of the green bird
Had flown from your mouth.

NIGHT
(for Hilary)

Love, let us lie
While the centuries stir
Sadly again,
In an uneasy air.

Once more men cry
For war, as though insane;
And now truths blur,
Now maps are threats of pain.

Love, let us sleep
While all the world goes mad
For hollow pride:
And all it never had.

For thoughts are cheap
And history denied;
And all seems bad
As we perceive the slide

Of all mankind;
As we watch goodness fall
Into the hands
That use it like a ball.

Love, let your mind
And my mind dock in lands
Where hate can't call:
And there are no demands.

Love, let us go
Like children put to bed.
For madmen wait
To cut Time's taut, thin thread.

Who will shout, 'No!'
Before it's all too late?
And there are dead
At the feet of the 'Great'?

Love, let us rest
Through darkness until light.
For all is blessed;
Even the nervous day
Now gone away:
Even this strange, strange, night.

CASTLE GARDENS, SWANSEA:
CHRISTMAS EVE

In the park, Christmas Eve,
A woman shares her lunch
With a throbbing puddle
Of pigeons at her feet.

POEMS FOR CHILDREN

THE LOCH NESS MONSTER
(for Molly)

The Loch Ness Monster is a myth;
Is the loch without? Or is it with?

If Nessie's there, why can't we see
A hump or two—or maybe three!

I WANT TO BE AN ASTRONAUT

I want to be an astronaut
And shoot off into space;
I want to float like a silver bird
Above the human race.

I want to ride a rocket,
Computerised (with lights);
I want to go beyond the stars
I've seen on winter nights.

I want the Earth to watch me
On their T.V. screens;
I want them all to see me go
Amongst fantastic scenes.

I want to be an astronaut
And go to Saturn soon;
I want to step down onto Mars
And the dark side of the Moon.

I want to spend my holidays
In a rocket that I'll fly;
I want to be an astronaut
Who waves our world goodbye.

I want to see the other worlds
And boys that aren't like me:
I want to see the strangest lands
And still be home for tea.

POETRY

Poetry
Is rhythm,
Poetry
Is the beat,
Poetry
Is the twitch
In your feet;
Poetry
Is sadness,
Poetry
Is a smile,
Poetry
Is your walk,
Poetry
Is your style,
Poetry
Is disco,
Poetry
Is the Blues,
Poetry
Is your socks
In your shoes;
Poetry
Is the sun,
Poetry
Is the rain,
Poetry
Is the joy,
Poetry
Is the pain;
Poetry
Is the sky,
Poetry
Is the sea,
Poetry
Is you, friend:
And it's me!

SPRING

Spring is a lamb l ^{e} ^{a} ^{p} ^{i}
                n   g

Spring is a breeze b l o w i n g

       g
       n
       i
       w
       o
       r
Spring is a flower g

Spring is a cat c . . . r . . . e . . . e . . . p . . . i . . . n . . . g

SOME PEOPLE IN OTHER LANDS

Some people in other lands
Hold begging bowls in their hands;

They have no drinks, they have no bread;
The sun burns hope inside each head.

Let's close our eyes, let's link our hands
And think of those in other lands.

SNOW

Snowfall,
Friends call.
Streets white,
So bright.
Cars stuck—
Bad luck!
Ice slide,
Sleigh ride.
Palm snow,
Ball throw.
Breath smokes;
Fun, jokes.
Great plan,
Make man,
Build high—
Grey sky.
Body, head,
Hat's red,
Nose black,
Mouth crack,
Coal eyes.
Happy cries!
In park,
Dogs bark;
Play chase—
Wet face!
Day's old:
Hungry, cold.
Some slush:
Can't rush.
Home go—
Love snow!

ONE SHEPHERD

And one shepherd, full of himself,
Did not go.
He remained in the field,
Feeling the black winter
As bitter and cold as his thoughts;
While the other shepherds
Were humbled by the warmth,
Like sunlight,
Surrounding the world's child.

COMMENTS ON *BALLAD OF KILVEY HILL*

In this new collection, Kilvey Hill dominates the poet's strong imagination, the landscape and the place are extremely important to him. It is an area east of Swansea where he grew up and is that famous ugly side, once known for its copper production and the docklands from where it was exported throughout the world. There are poems here which focus the eyes and freshen understanding as he writes with compassion and honesty in a lucid and individual voice . . . He has a natural, unsentimental love for the eastside of the city which has fuelled his imagination and by reading these poems we share his unique view of a specific place, depicting in words the mood and texture of the landscape . . . Readers interested in fine writing, set in a particular landscape should read this book for its controlled human emotion.

—**Byron Beynon,** Swansea poet and reviewer

In *Ballad of Kilvey Hill* we see Peter Thabit Jones as prospector, plunging fearlessly into the territory of Dylan Thomas' "ugly, lovely town" and claiming the Eastside corner as his rightful kingdom—"spread out in its poverty and its poetry" ("Summer"). Kilvey has a sturdy champion in Thabit Jones, whose poems and prose-poems celebrate the flawed, rough-hewn charm of an area not intrinsically lovely, but of limitless possibility in the eyes of a small boy . . . But it is the looming spectre of the hill itself which captures the imagination; of poet and reader alike . . . Despite the frequently stark portrait painted of the area that shaped his formative years—"like something out of Lowry's drab past"—Thabit Jones proves himself a poet of rare colour.

—**Sarah Smith,** reviewer

ACKNOWLEDGMENTS

to the following magazines and newspapers:

Austria/*The Poet's Voice* (University of Saltzburg); England/*Apostrophe, The Argotist, At Last, The Banshee, The Bound Spiral, Candelabrum, Eavesdropper, Exile, Foolscap, The Haiku Quarterly, Helicon, Iota, Krax, Lateral Moves, Outposts, Orbis, Peace and Freedom, Pennine Platform, Poetry and Audience, Poetry Nottingham, Poetry Review, Quartz, The Rialto, Roads, Rustic Rub, Samphire, Staple, Sol, T.O.P.S, Urbane Gorilla, Various Artists, Weyfarers, White Rose;* Scotland/*Northwords, Poetry Scotland, Understanding;* Switzerland/*2Plus2*; U.S.A./*Cumberland Poetry Review, New England Review/Bread Loaf Quarterly, Ninnau* (Welsh/American newspaper); Wales/*The Anglo-Welsh Review, Asp, Evening Post, Madog, Momentum, Planet, Poetry Wales, Western Mail.*

to the following anthologies and Teachers' Resources:

Australia/ *Cityscapes: A Reading Programme* (Scholastic Publications); England/ *Positively Poetry* (New Hope International); India/ *Parnassus of World Poets* (Parnassus); South Africa/ *Breaking the Poetry Barrier* (Heinemann-Centaur), *Let's Use English* (Heinemann International); United Kingdom/ *All in the Family* (Oxford University Press), *Changing Islands* (University Tutorial Press), *A Christmas Stocking* (Cassell Educational Ltd.), *Co-op U.K. Poetry Festival* (Co-op Ltd.), *Drama Links* (Hodder and Stoughton), *Families: Poems/Photographs* (Philip Green Educational), *Family Poems* (Scholastic Publications), *I Gave My Love a Red, Red Nose* (Franklyn Watts), *National Poetry Competition Prizewinners' Anthology* (The Poetry Society/Radio 3), *New Poetry 1* (Arts Council of Great Britain), *The Oxford Treasury of Christmas Poems* (Oxford University Press), *The Puffin Book of Christmas Poems* (Puffin/Penguin), *Reading Comprehension Book 5* (Macmillan Education), *Scholastic Collections: Poetry* (Scholastic Publications), *A Shooting Star* (Blackwell Education), *You Just Can't Win* (Penguin); Wales/ *Burning the Bracken* (Seren Books), *Green Horse* (Arts Council of Wales), *Poem Broadsheets* (Welsh Joint Education Committee), *The Poet's House* (Pont Books), *Red Poets: Numbers 1, 2, 4,* and *8* (Y Faner Goch), *A Swansea Anthology* (Seren Books), *Thoughts Like an Ocean* (Pont Books).

Others

"Garden of Ivy" and "The Boy" were runner-up poems in the National Poetry Competition, organized by The Poetry Society and BBC Radio 3, U.K.;

"Harry Pushed Her" was broadcast on *Rhymes and Riddles of Wales,* Radio Cymru, Wales; it was also included in the *1994 Children in Wales / Children in Scotland / National Children's Bureau* (U.K.) Annual Report (to mark International Year of the Family);

Some of the poems were part of two exhibitions, *Eastside Swansea* (at County Hall, Swansea, Wales) and *Ballad of Kilvey Hill* (at Swansea Central Library, Wales), with paintings by Nick Holly. The latter exhibition was featured on HTV Wales's television programme *Primetime Diary.*

Some poems were published in the following books by Peter Thabit Jones: Wales/ *Visitors* (Seren Books); U.K./ *Ballad of Kilvey Hill* (Swansea Bay Publishers / Eastside Poetry), *Clocks Tick Differently* (Celtion Poetry Series), *The Cold Cold Corner* (Dark Lane Poetry), *Tacky Brow* (Outposts Publications).

ABOUT THE ARTIST

Nick Holly, born in 1968, was brought up in the district of St Thomas on the industrial eastside of Swansea. He studied at Swansea College of Art and Design. His first exhibition with his gallery was in 1989, and since then he has been a regular exhibitor. As his work has developed, so has his reputation as a chronicler of the urban and industrial landscape of South Wales and, in particular, the community within which he still lives.

ARTWORK BY NICK HOLLY IN THIS VOLUME

Cover: *The Lizard Catchers #1,* colorized mixed-media on paper,
   9 1/4" x 6 1/4", 2003
   8: *The Lizard Catchers #1,* black & white mixed-media on paper,
   9 1/4" x 6 1/4", 2003
   50: *The Lizard Catchers #2,* black & white mixed-media on paper,
   9 1/4" x 6 1/4", 2003

ABOUT THE AUTHOR

Peter Thabit Jones was born in Swansea, Wales, U.K., in 1951. His work, particularly his poetry for children, has been featured in books by such publishers as Penguin, Puffin, Letts Education, Macmillan Education, Heinemann Educational, Oxford University Press, Simon and Schuster, Heinemann-Centaur (South Africa), and Scholastic Publications (Australia). It has also been featured on British television (HTV Wales), BBC Radio, and Educational Cassettes and has been published in many magazines and newspapers, including *Poetry Review* (U.K.), *Child Education* (U.K/Commonwealth), *New England Review* (U.S.A.), *Junior Education* (U.K./Commonwealth), *2Plus2* (Switzerland), *Poetry Wales* (U.K.), *Cumberland Poetry Review* (U.S.A.), *Ninnau* (U.S.A./Welsh newspaper). Peter's poetry is also included in *The New Companion to the Literature of Wales,* the literature chapters of two history books on Swansea, and a book on Dylan Thomas's Swansea. He is the recipient of several awards for his work, including the Eric Gregory Award for Poetry, The Society of Authors Award, The Royal Literary Fund Award (London, U.K.), and an Arts Council of Wales Award. In addition to this first book of his poetry published in America, *The Lizard Catchers,* he is the author of six other collections of poetry and one collection of short stories. Alan Llwyd, who scripted the Oscar-nominated Welsh-language film *Hedd Wyn,* once said, "[Peter] is a master of the exact word." Peter is also on the U.K. Author List of Heinemann Educational (Teaching Resources) and teaches five courses—including "Writing Children's Literature" and "Poets and Poetry"—at the University of Wales Swansea's Adult Educational Department. In November 1997, he visited America for ten days to give readings to organizations and schools in New York and New Jersey. He was commissioned by the *Western Mail,* the national newspaper of Wales, to write four pieces entitled "Postcard from New York." They covered his schedule and his stay at the Chelsea Hotel, where Dylan Thomas stayed prior to his death, and an interview with David Slivka, the sculptor who made Thomas's death mask.